## Play Time

# Let's Play Jacks

## By Sarah Hughes

Welcome
Books

Children's Press
A Division of Grolier Publishing
New York / London / Hong Kong / Sydney
Danbury, Connecticut

Photo Credits: Cover and all photos by Thaddeus Harden
Contributing Editor: Mark Beyer
Book Design: Michael DeLisio

Visit Children's Press on the Internet at:
http://publishing.grolier.com

Library of Congress Cataloging-in-Publication Data

Hughes, Sarah, 1964-
  Let's play jacks / by Sarah Hughes.
    p. cm. — (Play time)
  Includes bibliographical references and index.
  Summary: Simple text and photographs explain the game of jacks.
  ISBN 0-516-23113-8 (lib. bdg.) — ISBN 0-516-23038-7 (pbk.)
  1. Jacks (Game)—Juvenile literature. [1. Jacks (Game) 2. Games.] I. Title.

GV1215.7.H84
796.2—dc21

00-023356

# Contents

Sally, Petra, and Lynn like to play **jacks**.

They need a ball and ten jacks to play.

Petra throws the jacks onto the floor.

5

Petra throws the ball into the air.

She picks up only one jack.

Petra catches the ball before it **bounces** twice.

Each turn, Petra picks up one jack at a time.

She plays until all the jacks are picked up.

Now it is time for **twosies**.

Petra throws down the jacks.

She must pick up two at a time.

She can only let the ball bounce once.

Petra loses her turn if the ball bounces twice.

Now Lynn must start at **onesies**.

13

Lynn has finished with onesies and twosies.

She is now on **threesies.**

She lets the ball bounce only once.

She picks up three jacks at a time.

Finishing threesies leaves one **extra** jack.

This last jack is called the **cart**.

Lynn bounces the ball and picks up the last jack.

The girls must play up to ten to win.

Grabbing all ten jacks is hard.

Sally has grabbed ten jacks.

She catches the ball before it bounces twice.

Sally wins!

# New Words

**bounces** (**bowns**-ez) to spring back like a ball

**cart** (**kart**) the extra jack that is left after a turn

**extra** (**eks**-tra) more than is needed

**jacks** (**jaks**) small metal pieces that are star shaped

**onesies** (**wuhn**-zeez) when a player picks up one jack with each bounce of the ball

**threesies** (**three**-zeez) when a player picks up three jacks with each bounce of the ball

**twosies** (**too**-zeez) when a player picks up two jacks with each bounce of the ball

# To Find Out More

**Books**

*Jacks and More Jacks*
by Babs Bell Hajdusiewicz
Goodyear Publishing Company

*Jacks Around the World*
by Mary D. Lankford
William Morrow & Company

**Web Sites**

**Games Kids Play**
http://www.gameskidsplay.net
This page has a list of many games that kids can play. It also teaches how to play each game.

**Jacks**
http://www.primefun.com/jacks.htm
This site teaches all about how to play the game of jacks.

# Index

ball, 4, 6, 10, 12,
14, 16, 20

bounces, 6, 12,
16, 20

cart, 16

extra, 16

jack(s), 4, 6, 8, 10,
14, 16, 18, 20

onesies, 12, 14

threesies, 14, 16

twosies, 10, 14

## About the Author

Sarah Hughes is from New York City and taught school for twelve years. She is now writing and editing children's books. In her free time she enjoys running and riding her bike.

## Reading Consultants

Kris Flynn, Coordinator, Small School District Literacy, The San Diego County Office of Education

Shelly Forys, Certified Reading Recovery Specialist, W.J. Zahnow Elementary School, Waterloo, IL

Peggy McNamara, Professor, Bank Street College of Education, Reading and Literacy Program